✦ 50 WORDS ✦
ABOUT NATURE
PLANTS

TARA PEGLEY-STANGER

DEBBIE POWELL

OXFORD
UNIVERSITY PRESS

Note to Grown-ups

Learning lots of new words is a wonderful aid for young children's language development. A wide vocabulary also helps children to explore and understand the world around them as they grow and learn. Reading the words while looking at the pictures together creates a valuable learning experience.

This book includes new words as well as familiar ones. Even grown-ups might not know some of the words, and there is a pronunciation guide at the end of the book to help.

In this book you will find **50 words** about **plants**. There are many different kinds of plant, and we couldn't live without them! Keep reading to find out about plants with **spikes**, **leaves**, **flowers** and **fruit**, and the very **tallest trees**.

Plants are living things that grow on land and in water.

Plants grow almost everywhere on planet Earth.

They can be huge, like an **oak tree** ...

... or tiny, like a **daisy**.

The **peony** is a plant you might have seen in a park or garden.

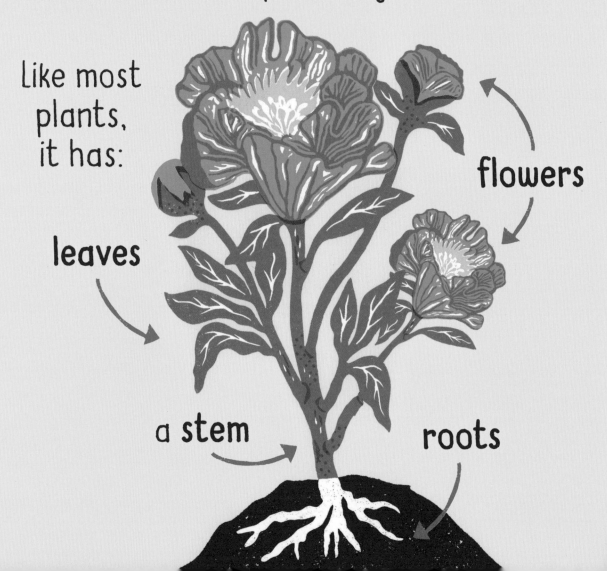

Like most plants, it has:

flowers

leaves

a stem

roots

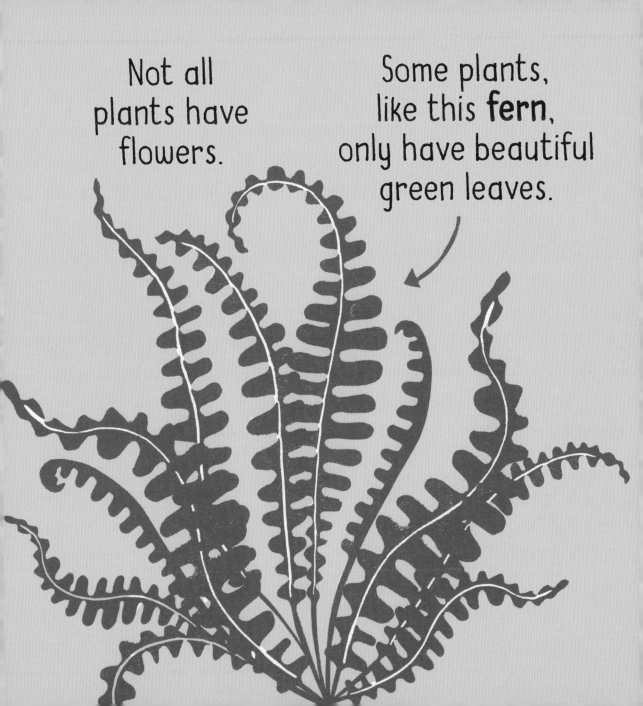

Plants make energy
in a process called
photosynthesis.

Green **chlorophyll** in
their leaves stores sunlight.

They use sunlight to make sugar, which gives them the energy to grow.

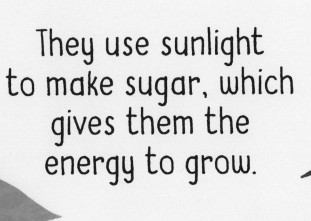

As part of photosynthesis, plants release the gas **oxygen**, which all animals need to breathe.

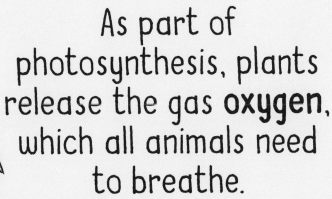

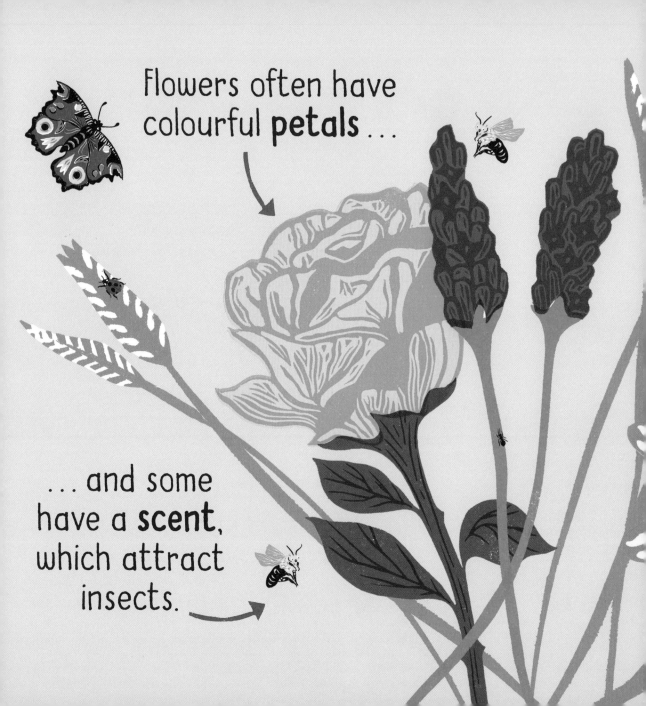

Flowers often have colourful **petals**...

...and some have a **scent**, which attract insects.

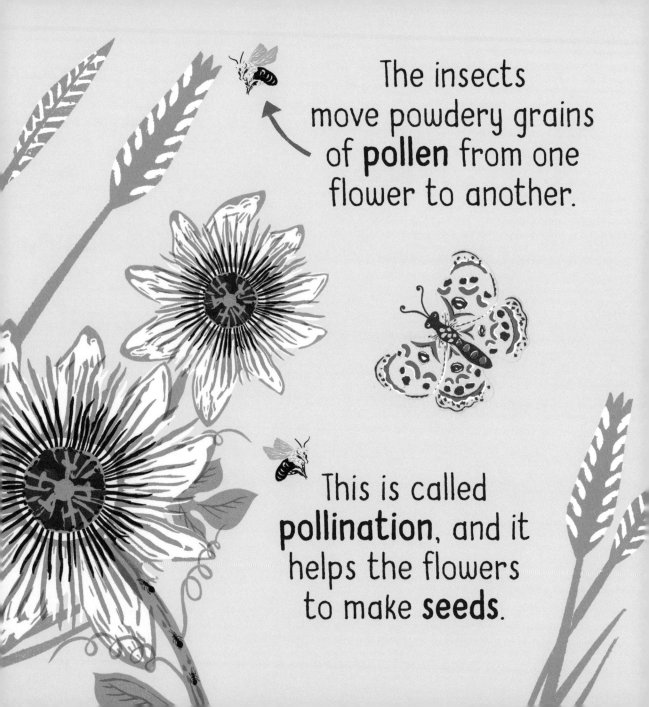

The insects move powdery grains of **pollen** from one flower to another.

This is called **pollination**, and it helps the flowers to make **seeds**.

Flowering plants produce **fruits**, which contain seeds.

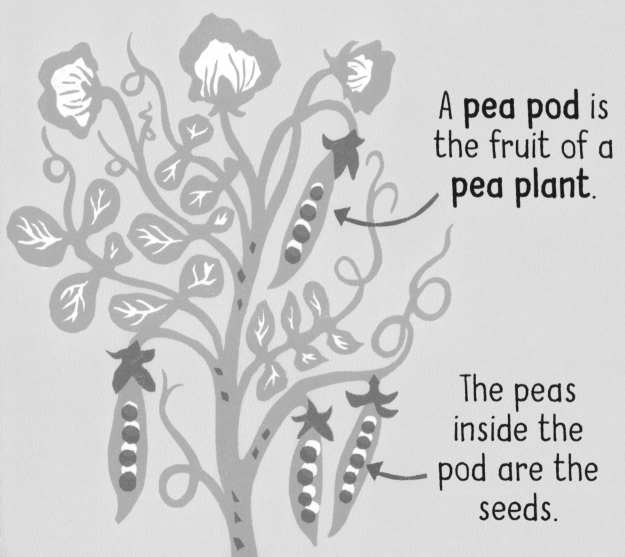

A **pea pod** is the fruit of a **pea plant**.

The peas inside the pod are the seeds.

Some fruits are tasty,
like **grapes**, or these
strawberries.

Birds
and other
animals eat
the fruit and
spread the
seeds in their
droppings.

Some types of
new plants grow
from seeds.

When a seed begins to grow,
or **germinates**, the hard
case breaks open.

Roots grow down
into the **soil**.

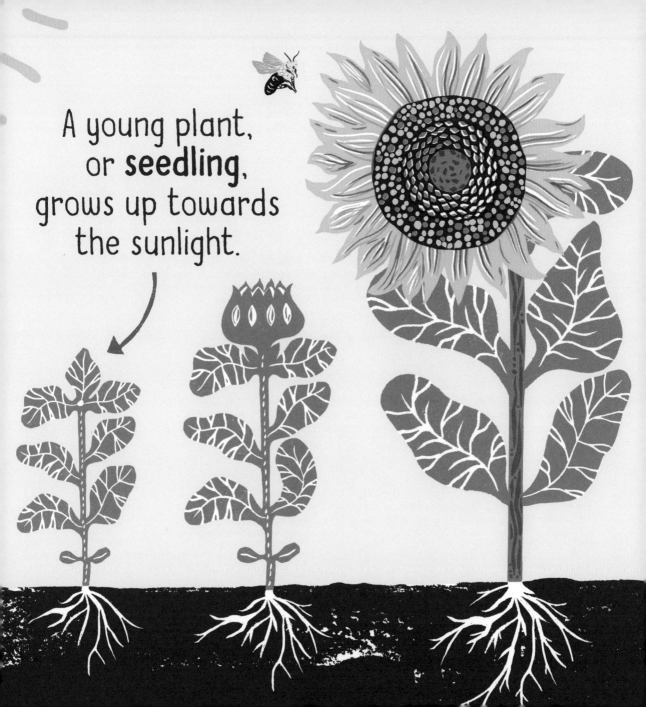

A young plant, or **seedling**, grows up towards the sunlight.

Tropical rainforests are warm, damp places full of plants and animals.

The **canopy** is the main layer of tree tops.

The tallest **trees** are called **emergents**.

The **understorey** includes younger trees.

On the **forest floor**, there is very little light.

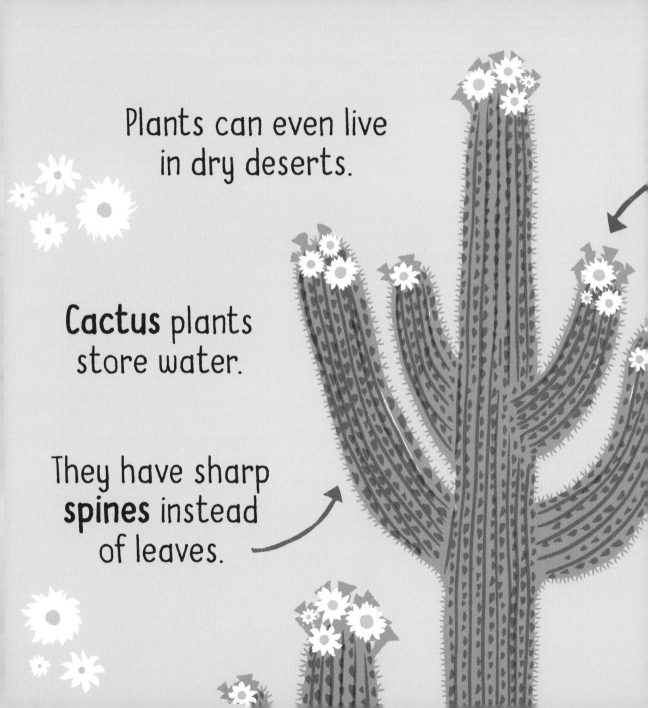

Plants can even live
in dry deserts.

Cactus plants
store water.

They have sharp
spines instead
of leaves.

Cacti are flowering plants.

This **saguaro cactus** has white-and-yellow flowers.

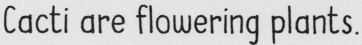

After flowering, this **prickly pear** produces tasty fruit.

Some plants live in water–they
are **aquatic plants**.

This **water lily**'s
roots reach
into the bottom
of a river or
pond ...

... and
its leaves
float on the
surface.

Water lettuce plants float in the water.

Other plants live underwater completely, like this **water milfoil**.

Trees are the tallest plants.

Some are **deciduous** –they lose their leaves in winter.

Some trees are **evergreen**, like this one— they keep their leaves all year round.

Conifers produce **cones**. Seeds form inside the cones.

This **coast redwood** is a **conifer**. It is the tallest tree in the world.

People cannot live without plants.

We eat fruit,
such as **apples**.

And **vegetables**,
such as **spinach**
or **carrots**.

We make bread
from **wheat**,
a type of **grass**.

We use plants to make clothes, furniture, buildings, and even medicine.

Plants make the oxygen we breathe. And they make us feel good!

People who study plants
are called **botanists**.

They learn about
how plants grow,
where they live,
and the homes they
provide for animals.

50 WORDS

ABOUT NATURE

PLANTS

TARA PEGLEY-STANGER

DEBBIE POWELL

OXFORD
UNIVERSITY PRESS

Note to Grown-ups

Learning lots of new words is a wonderful aid for young children's language development. A wide vocabulary also helps children to explore and understand the world around them as they grow and learn. Reading the words while looking at the pictures together creates a valuable learning experience.

This book includes new words as well as familiar ones. Even grown-ups might not know some of the words, and there is a pronunciation guide at the end of the book to help.

In this book you will find **50 words** about **plants**. There are many different kinds of plant, and we couldn't live without them! Keep reading to find out about plants with **spikes**, **leaves**, **flowers** and **fruit**, and the very **tallest trees**.

Plants are living things that grow on land and in water.

Plants grow almost everywhere on planet Earth.

... or tiny,
like a **daisy**.

They can
be huge, like an
oak tree ...

Most have
underground roots.

The **peony** is a plant you might have seen in a park or garden.

Like most plants, it has:

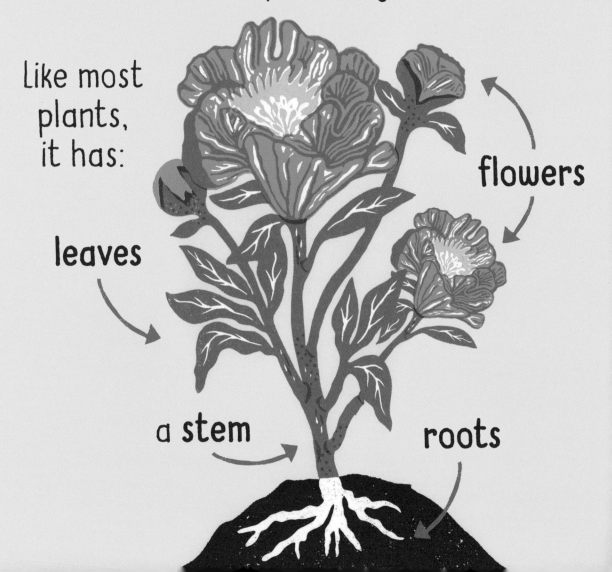

flowers

leaves

a stem

roots

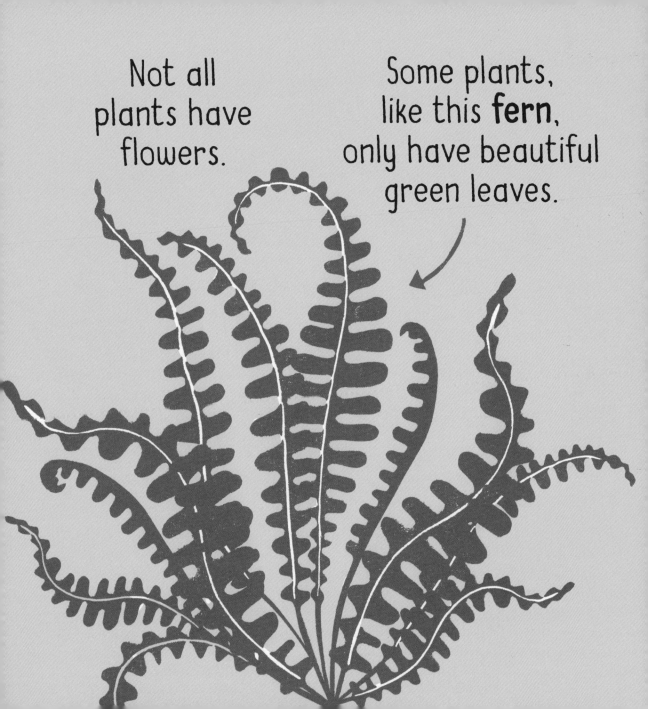

Not all plants have flowers.

Some plants, like this **fern**, only have beautiful green leaves.

Plants make energy
in a process called
photosynthesis.

Green **chlorophyll** in
their leaves stores sunlight.

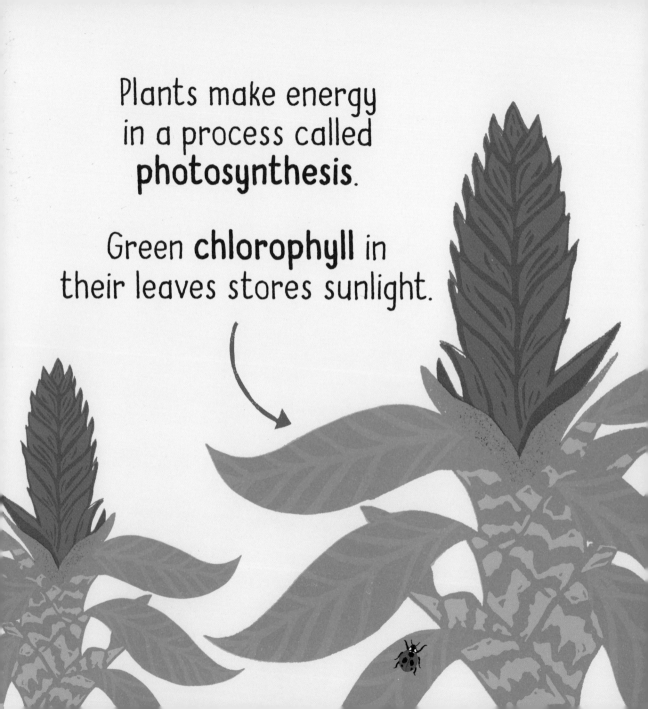

They use sunlight
to make sugar, which
gives them the
energy to grow.

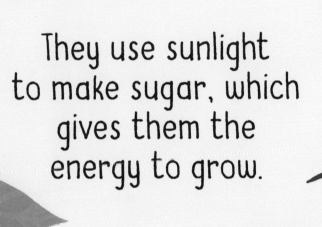

As part of
photosynthesis, plants
release the gas **oxygen**,
which all animals need
to breathe.

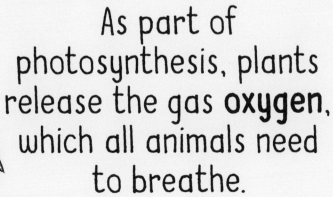

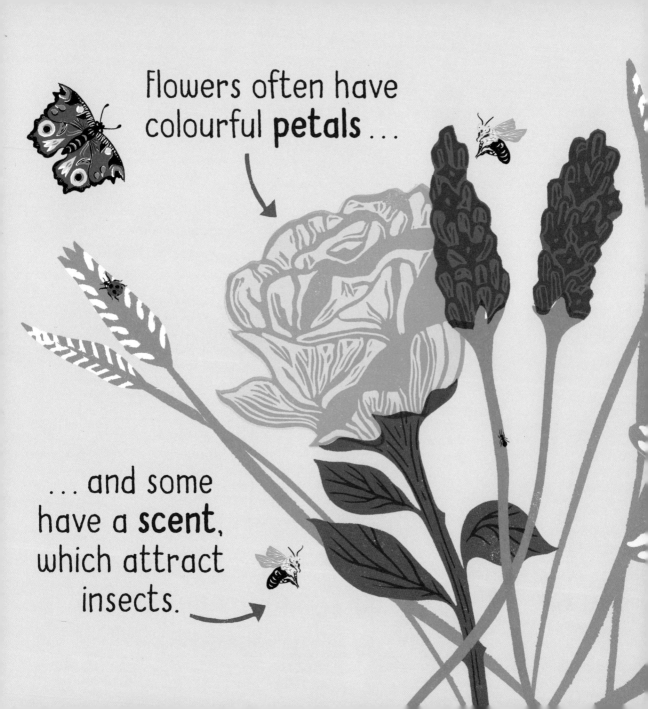

Flowers often have colourful **petals** ...

... and some have a **scent**, which attract insects.

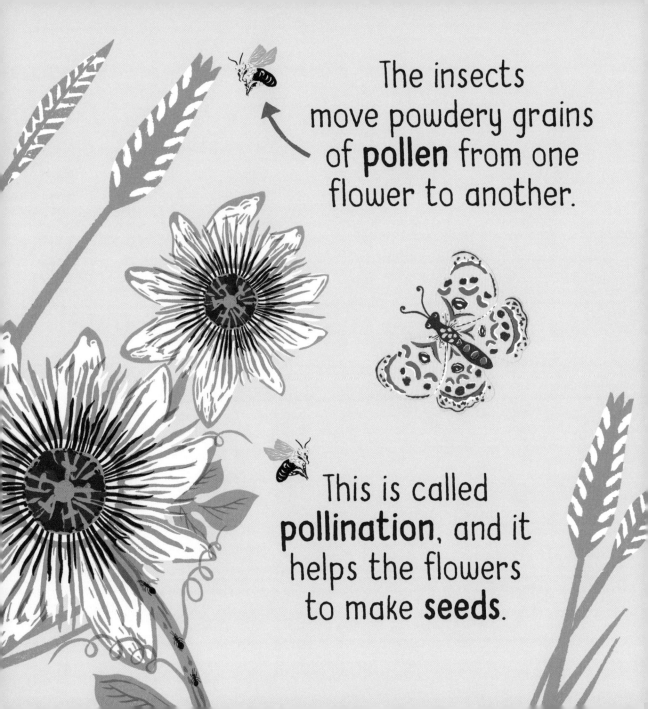

The insects move powdery grains of **pollen** from one flower to another.

This is called **pollination**, and it helps the flowers to make **seeds**.

Flowering plants produce **fruits**, which contain seeds.

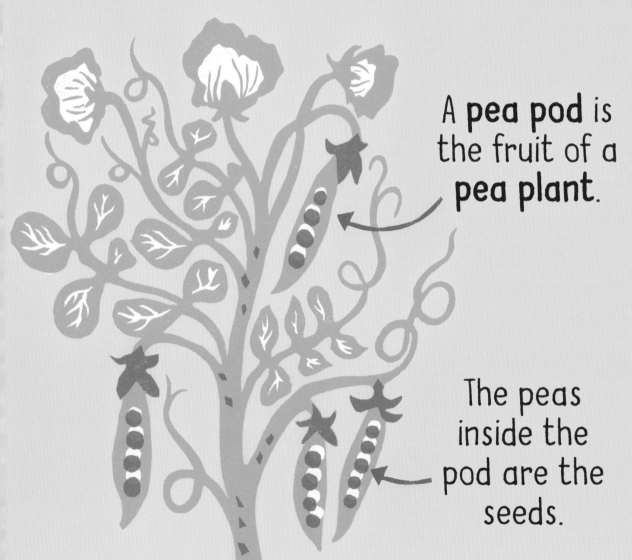

A **pea pod** is the fruit of a **pea plant**.

The peas inside the pod are the seeds.

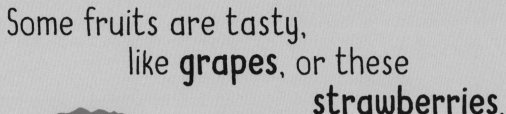

Some fruits are tasty,
like **grapes**, or these
strawberries.

Birds
and other
animals eat
the fruit and
spread the
seeds in their
droppings.

Some types of
new plants grow
from seeds.

When a seed begins to grow,
or **germinates**, the hard
case breaks open.

Roots grow down
into the **soil**.

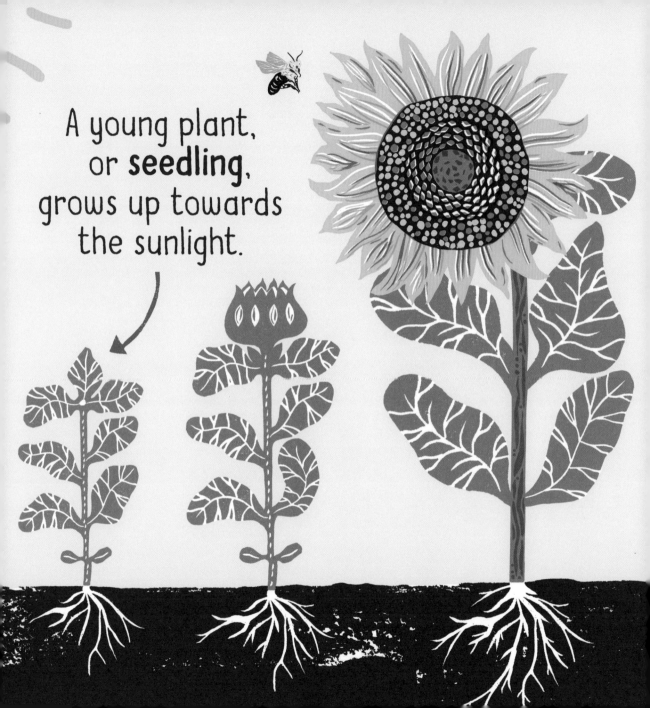

A young plant,
or **seedling**,
grows up towards
the sunlight.

Tropical **rainforests** are warm, damp places full of plants and animals.

The **canopy** is the main layer of tree tops.

The tallest **trees** are called **emergents**.

The **understorey** includes younger trees.

On the **forest floor**, there is very little light.

Plants can even live in dry deserts.

Cactus plants store water.

They have sharp **spines** instead of leaves.

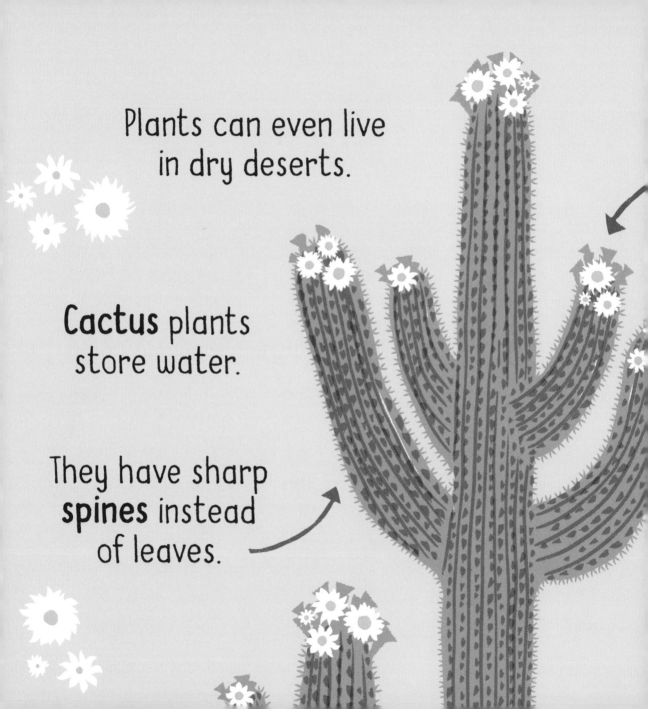

Cacti are flowering plants.

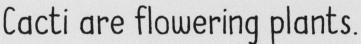

This **saguaro cactus** has white-and-yellow flowers.

After flowering, this **prickly pear** produces tasty fruit.

Some plants live in water—they are **aquatic plants**.

This **water lily**'s roots reach into the bottom of a river or pond...

... and its leaves float on the surface.

Water lettuce plants float in the water.

Other plants live underwater completely, like this **water milfoil**.

Trees are the tallest plants.

Some are **deciduous** –they lose their leaves in winter.

Some trees are **evergreen**, like this one— they keep their leaves all year round.

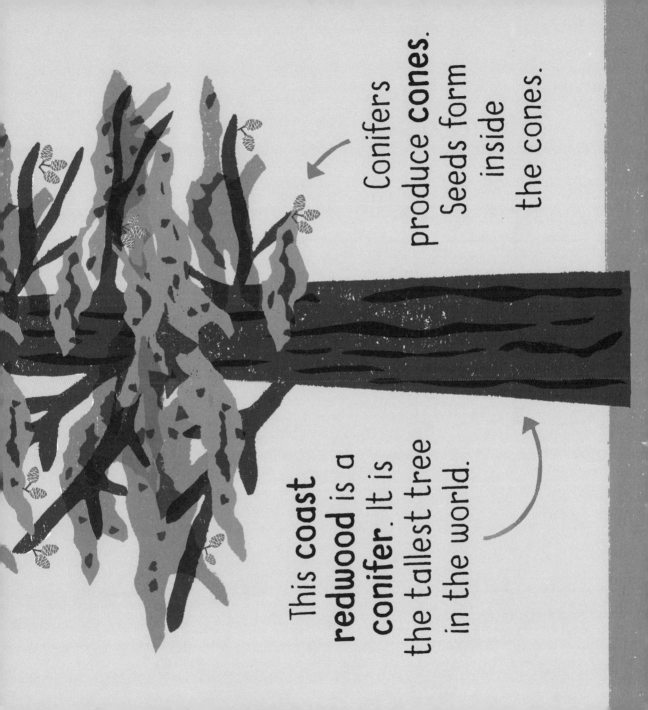

Conifers produce **cones**. Seeds form inside the cones.

This **coast redwood** is a **conifer**. It is the tallest tree in the world.

People cannot live without plants.

We eat fruit,
such as **apples**.

And **vegetables**,
such as **spinach**
or **carrots**.

We make bread
from **wheat**,
a type of **grass**.

We use plants to make clothes, furniture, buildings, and even medicine.

Plants make the oxygen we breathe. And they make us feel good!

People who study plants
are called **botanists**.

They learn about
how plants grow,
where they live,
and the homes they
provide for animals.

This is one of the plants botanists have discovered recently.

It's found in Cameroon, and is very rare.

vine

edible

You could be like a
botanist and learn
more about plants.

Ask for help to plant
a seed, then watch
it grow.

tendril

bloom

How many other
words about plants
do you know?

herb

lavender